SAMMY SOSA

A Real-Life Reader Biography

Carrie Muskat

Mitchell Lane Publishers, Inc.
P.O. Box 619 • Bear, Delaware 19701

Real-Life Reader Biographies

Selena	Robert Rodriguez	Mariah Carey	Rafael Palmeiro
Tommy Nuñez	Trent Dimas	Cristina Saralegui	Andres Galarraga
Oscar De La Hoya	Gloria Estefan	Jimmy Smits	Mary Joe Fernandez
Cesar Chavez	Chuck Norris	Sinbad	Paula Abdul
Vanessa Williams	Celine Dion	Mia Hamm	**Sammy Sosa**
Brandy	Michelle Kwan	Rosie O'Donnell	Shania Twain
Garth Brooks	Jeff Gordon	Mark McGwire	Salma Hayek
Sheila E.	Hollywood Hogan	Ricky Martin	Britney Spears
Arnold Schwarzenegger	Jennifer Lopez	Kobe Bryant	Derek Jeter
Steve Jobs	Sandra Bullock	Julia Roberts	Robin Williams
Jennifer Love Hewitt	Keri Russell	Sarah Michelle Gellar	Liv Tyler
Melissa Joan Hart	Drew Barrymore	Alicia Silverstone	Katie Holmes
Winona Ryder	Alyssa Milano	Freddie Prinze, Jr.	Enrique Iglesias
Christina Aguilera			

Library of Congress Cataloging-in-Publication Data
Muskat, Carrie.
    Sammy Sosa/Carrie Muskat.
        p. cm. — (A real-life reader biography)
    Includes index.
    Summary: Presents the life and baseball career of the Dominican-born slugger who, along with Mark McGwire, in 1998 broke the long-standing record of most home runs hit in a season.
    ISBN 1-883845-96-3 (lib. bdg.)
    1. Sosa, Sammy, 1968- Juvenile literature. 2. Baseball players—Dominican Republic Biography Juvenile literature. [1. Sosa, Sammy, 1968- . 2. Baseball players. 3. Dominicans (Dominican Republic) Biography.] I Title. II. Series.
GV865.S59M89 1999
796.357'092—dc21
[B]
               99-19951
               CIP

ABOUT THE AUTHOR: Carrie Muskat has covered major league baseball since 1981, beginning with United Press International in Minneapolis. She was UPI's lead writer at the 1991 World Series. A freelance journalist since 1992, she is a regular contributor to *USA Today* and *USA Today Baseball Weekly.* Her work has appeared in the *Chicago Tribune, Inside Sports,* and *ESPN Total Sports* magazine. She is the author of several baseball books for children, including *Barry Bonds* (Chelsea House), *Moises Alou* (Mitchell Lane), and *Mark McGwire* (Chelsea House). She started interviewing and writing about Sammy Sosa when he joined the White Sox in July 1989. She has been to Comiskey Park and Wrigley Field for almost every home game since 1987.

PHOTO CREDITS: cover: Sporting News/Archive photos; pp. 4, 7, 11, 13, 29 Carrie Muskat; p. 18 Allsport; p. 21 Tim Brokema/Allsport; pp. 24, 26, 27 AP Photo.

ACKNOWLEDGMENTS: The following story was developed based on personal interviews with Sammy Sosa from 1989 through 1998. The author has intimate knowledge of the facts contained in this book and has twice been to the Dominican Republic (1996 and 1998) to report on Sammy's life there. However, this book is neither authorized nor endorsed by Sammy Sosa or any of his representatives. This story has been thoroughly researched and checked for accuracy. To the best of our knowledge, it represents a true story.

Table of Contents

Chapter 1
Shoeshine Boy

In the summer of 1998, two baseball players drew the attention of nearly everyone in the United States. The two men were trying to break one of baseball's most important records: the single-season home-run mark. Thirty-seven years earlier, Roger Maris had belted 61 home runs, one more than Babe Ruth's record set in 1927. Now Mark McGwire was closing in on Maris's record. McGwire had nearly broken the mark the season before, when he hit 58 homers, so baseball fans were expecting him to come close again.

Two men were trying to break one of baseball's most important records.

Sosa finished the season with 66 homers.

However, at the start of the season few fans expected Chicago Cubs' outfielder Sammy Sosa to also be in pursuit of the home-run record. Sosa had set a major-league record by hitting 20 home runs in June 1998. That put him on track to break the record, and he continued chasing McGwire through July and August. On September 8, McGwire became the first player to hit 62 home runs in the major leagues. Fittingly, it was a game against the Cubs, and the red-headed slugger hugged Sosa after hitting the historic, record-breaking home run.

Sosa finished the season with 66 homers—five more than the old record, but four behind McGwire. Even though he didn't win the home-run race, he was elected the National League's Most Valuable Player because of his .308 batting average, 158 runs batted in, and his role in helping the Cubs into the playoffs for the first time in nine years. More importantly, the classy way that the Latin American hitter handled all the hoopla surrounding the home-run race was admired by many people throughout the United States.

Sammy Sosa was born on November 12, 1968. He was the fifth child of six born to Lucrecia and Inez Montero Sosa. The family lived in a town called San Pedro de Macoris, which is located in a tiny Caribbean country called the Dominican Republic.

When Sammy was seven years old, his father died, and Lucrecia had to bring up the children by herself. The family was very poor. They lived in a small two-room apartment. Sometimes, Sammy had to sleep on the floor because there was no room in the bed.

Sammy Sosa grew up in this small home in the Dominican Republic.

The children worked to bring home money for food. Sammy would shine shoes,

wash cars, or sell oranges—anything to help his family.

When the children were not busy with chores, they would play baseball in the street. They could not afford any equipment, so they would wrap tape around a rolled-up sock and use it for a ball. They would find a heavy stick to swing as a bat. Sammy cut a milk carton in half and used that as a glove.

Sammy had seen what happened when ballplayers from the Dominican Republic made it to the major leagues in the United States. They came home wearing fancy gold jewelry and beautiful clothes and they drove nice cars. They did not have to worry about food. "Those players, when they came home I saw they had everything," Sammy recalled. "They had all these people around them. They were like kings. I said I wanted to be like that."

Sammy had first trained to be a boxer but he stopped because of his mother. "She said if I ever make it, she'd never watch me," he explained.

His older brother Luis once had a tryout with a professional baseball team, but he was told that he was too small. Sammy had great athletic ability, so Luis encouraged his younger brother to try baseball. Sammy started playing organized baseball at the age of 14.

Two years later, Sammy was invited to a tryout in front of major league scouts. Because his family was so poor, he had not eaten well his entire life. As a result, Sammy did not have much strength. He hit weak ground balls and his throws from the outfield took two or three hops before they reached the infielder. But two scouts from the Texas Rangers, Amado Dinzey and Omar Minaya, saw that Sammy had potential. "The ball had life when he hit it—that's what impressed me," Minaya later said.

On July 30, 1985, Sammy signed his first professional baseball contract with the Rangers for $3,500. He was 16 years old.

Scouts from the Texas Rangers saw that Sammy had potential.

Chapter 2
Welcome to the USA

The Texas Rangers assigned Sammy to a rookie team.

Sammy's mother was worried about her son going to the United States. Sammy was excited because he was going to make money to help take care of his family. Four or five Latin players would share an apartment. Any extra money that they earned went home to their families.

The Texas Rangers assigned Sammy to a rookie team in the Gulf Coast League. Baseball was easy—the tough part was learning English. Sammy could only speak Spanish. He often ate at fast food restaurants. He would wait for one of his friends to order, and then nod and ask for the same thing.

Each year, Sammy took another step up in the Rangers' minor league system. During the off-season, he would return to the Dominican Republic to play winter baseball in the capital city, Santo Domingo. Sammy was getting stronger, and he had talent, but he needed to play as much as he could to improve his baseball skills.

At the start of the 1989 season, Sammy was assigned to Class AA Tulsa. He batted .297, his best average

Sammy with his mother Lucrecia

in the minor leagues. On June 16, 1989, the Rangers brought Sammy up to the major leagues. He had two hits in his first game, against the New York Yankees. Sammy hit his first major league home run five days later, off Boston pitcher Roger Clemens.

Sammy did not stay with the Rangers long. He was sent back to the minor leagues after 25 games. He would not stay there long, however.

Larry Himes, the general manager of the Chicago White Sox, saw Sammy play four games in the minors. He was impressed by Sammy's work habits. Every day, Sammy would take some baseballs and hit off a batting tee by himself. He really wanted to get better.

Himes liked the young outfielder's energy so much that he wanted him on his team. So, on July 29 the White Sox traded outfielder Harold Baines and infielder Fred Manrique to the Rangers for Sammy, pitcher Wilson Alvarez, and infielder Scott Fletcher.

Sammy was called up to the White Sox on August 22. His first game for his new big-league team was sensational. He had three hits in three at-bats, including a home run.

"He's a little rough around the edges, that's all," said Marv Foley, who managed Sammy at the White Sox organization's Class AAA team, Vancouver, for two weeks before Sammy was called up to the big leagues. "But he's got the potential to be a great one."

Sammy and a school boy flash Sammy's "I love you" sign that he gives after home runs.

Chapter 3
Tons of Talent

Sammy Sosa made a good first impression with the Chicago White Sox. He hit .273 average in 33 games in 1989, although he did make some mistakes on the field. "He's just getting comfortable on this level," White Sox manager Jeff Torborg said.

Baseball became difficult for Sammy in 1990. Walt Hriniak was the White Sox hitting coach. He wanted his hitters to adjust to his style. Sammy struggled. He hit just .233 with 15 home runs that season.

Sammy felt good when the 1991 season started, but soon things were worse than the year before. He was taken out of the White Sox starting lineup in late April. Sammy did not think he could get better unless he played.

His power was there. Sammy won two games in May with 12th-inning home runs. But he went back into a slump in June. The White Sox sent him down to their Triple-A Vancouver team in mid-July.

He was called back to the big leagues on August 27. "This time, I'll stay here forever," Sosa promised himself. "This time, I'm a better man and I'll do a better job." However, he ended the year hitting just .203. Some people thought he had not tried hard enough to conform to Hriniak's hitting style. Sammy did try, but he thought it was not fair to be asked to change his hitting style so drastically.

Although the White Sox seemed ready to give up on Sammy Sosa, Larry Himes, the man who had traded for Sosa in 1989, was not. Himes took a job

In 1991, Sammy ended the year hitting just .203.

with the Chicago Cubs after the 1991 season ended. He still thought Sammy was a talented ballplayer. Just one week before the 1992 regular season began, Himes traded for the young outfielder again. This time, he sent veteran outfielder George Bell to the White Sox in exchange for Sammy and pitcher Ken Patterson. Sammy had once washed Bell's cars in the Dominican Republic.

"He's got a lot of talent," White Sox general manager Ron Schueler said about Sammy when the trade was made. "One of these years, he's going to put it all together." Sammy was excited to be going to a new team, and hoped he would get a chance to prove himself with the Cubs.

Chapter 4
30-30 Seasons

Sammy was anxious to show the Chicago Cubs they had made the right move by trading for him. Injuries cut his season short in 1992. In June, he was hit by a pitch by Montreal's Dennis Martinez and suffered a broken right hand. He came back in late July and hit a home run on the first pitch he saw. Sammy's hand had apparently healed well.

But in the tenth game after his hand injury, Sammy fouled a pitch off his left ankle. Somehow, he got to his feet and stayed in the batter's box long enough to draw a walk. Then, he asked

Injuries cut Sammy's season short that year.

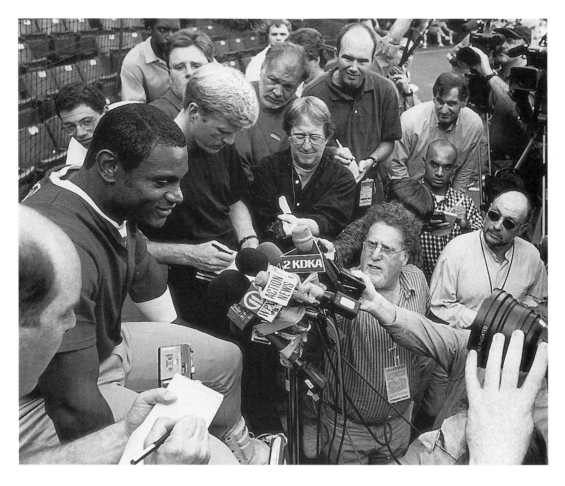

Sammy is friendly and cooperative with the media.

to be taken out of the game. X-rays showed a broken bone in his left ankle. "[I]t was a one-in-a-million freak accident," said Cubs trainer John Fierro. Sammy missed the remainder of the season.

The 1993 season meant a fresh start and Sammy finally put it all together in the major leagues. He became the first player in Cubs history to record a "30–30" season. Sammy finished with 33 homers and 36 stolen bases.

Sosa had another solid year in 1994. He won the Cubs' "triple crown," batting a career-high .300 with 25 homers and 70 RBI. His numbers would have been greater, but the major-league players went on strike on August 12 and the final six weeks of the season were canceled. In 1995, Sammy put together a second 30–30 season, totaling 36 home runs and 34 stolen bases. Being consistent was just what the Cubs wanted to see.

Sammy definitely had his power stroke going for him in 1996. He broke a window in an apartment building across the street from Wrigley Field with one of his home runs. He had 40 homers by August 20 when he was hit on the hand by a pitch by Florida's Mark Hutton. He stayed in the game four more innings

In 1993, Sammy became the first player in Cubs history to record a "30–30" season. He finished with 33 homers and 36 stolen bases.

before leaving. X-rays showed a clean break of a bone in his right hand. He was finished for the year. "I have to take it like a man," Sammy said. "This isn't the end to my career."

The 1997 season started badly both for Sammy and for his team. The Cubs had been expected to challenge for the National League Central title. Instead, the team started 0-14, and Sammy hit just .216. The team never recovered. Sammy finished with 36 home runs and 119 runs batted in, which equaled his career high. However, he hit just .251 and he struck out 174 times, the most in the National League.

The biggest day of 1997 for Sammy was June 27. On that day, Cubs officials announced they had signed him to a four-year, $42.5 million contract. The deal made him the third-highest paid player in baseball.

Sammy appreciated the confidence the Cubs had in him. "People always talk about the millions of dollars," he said. "This is not my type of thing.

On June 27, 1997, the Cubs signed Sammy to a four-year $42.5 million contract.

Money doesn't mean anything to me.
The only reason I'm here is because I
play good."

Sammy flashes his trademark victory sign.

Chapter 5
"Sammy, You're the Man"

In 1998, Sammy hit his first home run of the season on April 4 off Montreal's Marc Valdes.

In spring training 1998, Sammy and Cubs hitting coach Jeff Pentland set their goals for the season. Sammy wanted to hit .300. Pentland wanted Sammy to score 100 runs and walk 100 times. They did not talk about hitting home runs. "If I try," Sammy said, "I'll never get it because I'll overswing."

Sammy got off to a good start by batting .343 in April. He hit his first home run of the year on April 4 off Montreal's Marc Valdes. At the end of May, Sammy had 13 home runs. He was far behind the league leader, though. Mark McGwire, the powerful first baseman for the St. Louis Cardinals, had 27. McGwire was trying to break the major league record for most home runs in a single season: 61, set in 1961 by Roger Maris.

Sammy caught up to McGwire in June. Sammy set a major league record that month by hitting 20 home runs. That broke the old mark of 18, set in August 1937 by Detroit's Rudy York. "It's just so much fun to watch him," Pentland said of Sosa. "It's not supposed to be that easy."

On July 27 at Arizona, Sammy made personal history. He had hit 246 career home runs but had never hit one with the bases loaded. The Cubs loaded the bases in the eighth inning against Arizona pitcher Alan Embree. Sammy stepped into the batter's box and boom, he hit the first pitch high into right center field for his first career grand slam. To top it off, he hit his second grand slam the next day.

After every home run, Sammy would touch his heart and blow kisses

On July 27, 1998, Sammy hit his first grand slam ever. To top it off, he hit his second the next day.

St. Louis Cardinal first baseman Mark McGwire blows a Sammy Sosa kiss to the Chicago slugger after Sosa was walked on August 19, 1998. Sosa and McGwire both hit their 48th home runs during this game.

to his mother who was watching back in the Dominican Republic. In 1998, he also gave a "V" symbol in memory of the Cubs' popular broadcaster Harry Caray, who had died in February at the age of 84.

By mid-August, Sammy and McGwire were tied with 47 homers each. Sammy hit his 48th in the fifth inning August 19 against the Cardinals.

It was the first time he had the lead in their home-run race. However, Sammy's lead lasted less than an hour. McGwire hit a solo homer in the eighth and another in the 10th to go ahead again with 49. "That's why he is 'The Man,'" Sammy said of McGwire.

The Cubs celebrated Sammy's success with "Sammy Sosa Day" on September 20. Wrigley Field was decorated with flags from the Dominican Republic. Merengue music played and all of Sammy's family was present for the festivities. A big banner attached to the left field fence said, "Sammy: You're the Man."

On September 25, Sammy took the home run lead again when he hit his 66th. Forty-five minutes later, McGwire hit number 66 in a game between Montreal and St. Louis to tie Sammy. In the last week of the season, McGwire hit four more home runs to finish with 70.

Although Sammy had come up four short, finishing with 66, he had said all season long that reaching the

On August 19, Sammy took the lead in the home run race. However, his lead lasted less than an hour.

Sammy takes a victory lap around Wrigley field after "Sammy Sosa Day" festivities before the Cubs game against the Cincinnati Reds on September 20, 1998 in Chicago.

playoffs was more important than winning the home run title. He got his wish. The Cubs made it to the National League playoffs as the wild card entry, only to lose to Atlanta in three games.

Sammy did accomplish two of the three personal goals that he had set before the season began. He finished with a .308 batting average and scored 134 runs. He fell short of his goal of 100 walks—he had 73—but that was a career-high. He also led the league with 158 runs batted in. In all areas of his hitting, Sammy had shown tremendous improvement. Then in November, Sammy was voted the National League's Most Valuable Player (MVP). He received 30 of the 32 first-place votes and a total of 438 points in the balloting by the Baseball Writers' Association of America. Mark McGwire garnered second place and Moises Alou took third.

In 1998, Sammy hit one home run after another. It was an unbelievable season.

It was an unbelievable season. "Believe it," Sammy said.

Chapter 6
Sammy Claus

Sammy Sosa has a big heart. He always thinks about his family and his homeland, the Dominican Republic.

Sammy has a big heart.

In 1996, he contributed money to build the "30-30 Plaza" in his hometown. A medical clinic was established in the building. The plaza got its name from Sammy's two "30–30" seasons with the Chicago Cubs when he hit at least 30 homers and stole 30 bases.

He has also donated 250 computers to schools in the Dominican Republic, and when the city of San Pedro de Macoris needed an ambulance, he bought one.

"I'll never forget where I came from," Sammy said. "I'm proud of the United States. They've given me everything that I have. They gave me the opportunity to be Sammy Sosa today. But I have to remember that these are my people, people I have to take care of, people I have to give jobs to when I open the plaza. This is my life."

In the center of the 30-30 Plaza is a fountain with a statue of Sosa. It is called the *Fuente de los Limpia Botas,* the Fountain of the Shoeshine

In the center of the 30–30 Plaza is a fountain with a statue of Sammy Sosa. It is the fountain of the shoeshine boys.

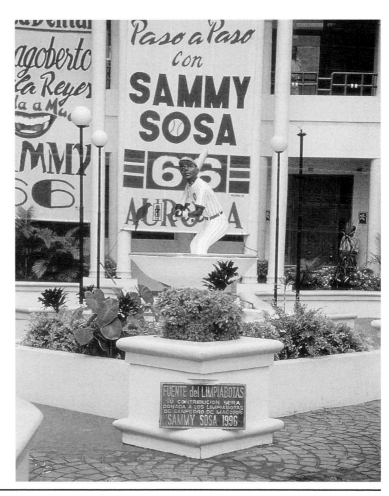

Boys. Sammy Sosa has never forgotten how he once shined shoes in the center of town. All money thrown into the fountain is given to the shoeshine boys in San Pedro de Macoris.

Sammy doesn't limit his charity to people in the Dominican Republic. In December 1997, he distributed more than 7,000 toys to children in schools and hospitals in seven cities on his "Sammy Claus" tour. He made stops in Washington, D.C., Philadelphia, New York, Chicago, Miami, San Pedro de Macoris, and Santo Domingo.

But his most ambitious challenge came in 1998. Hurricane Georges ravaged the Dominican Republic in late September. Hundreds of thousands of people were left homeless and Sosa dedicated himself to helping them rebuild. He organized a relief effort in the United States that sent money, clothes, and other essential supplies to the people who had lost everything in the storm. Sammy received a hero's

Sammy doesn't limit his charity to people in the Dominican Republic.

welcome in October when he finally returned home.

"I always say, he was chosen by God," his brother Juan said.

During Sammy's post-game news conference on "Sammy Sosa Day," September 20, 1998, someone asked the shoeshine boy-turned-home-run-hero about his next goal in life.

"Go to heaven," Sammy said.

It is a good goal to have.

Major League Stats

YR	TEAM	G	AB	R	H	2B	3B	HR	RBI	BB	AVG
1989	2TM	58	183	27	47	8	0	4	13	11	.257
	Tex	25	84	8	20	3	0	1	3	0	.238
	ChA	33	99	19	27	5	0	3	10	11	.273
1990	ChA	153	532	72	124	26	10	15	70	33	.233
1991	ChA	116	316	39	64	10	1	10	33	14	.203
1992	ChN	67	262	41	68	7	2	8	25	19	.260
1993	ChN	159	598	92	156	25	5	33	93	38	.261
1994	ChN	105	426	59	128	17	6	25	70	25	.300
1995	ChN	144	564	89	151	17	3	36	119	58	.268
1996	ChN	124	498	84	136	21	2	40	100	34	.273
1997	ChN	162	642	90	161	31	4	36	119	45	.251
1998	ChN	159	643	134	198	20	0	66	158	73	.308
1999	ChN	162	625	114	180	24	2	63	141	78	.288
2000	ChN	156	604	106	193	38	1	50	138	91	.320
TOTALS		1565	5893	947	1606	244	36	386	1079	519	.273

Chronology

Index